Orillia Ontario in Colour Photos, Saving Our History One Photo at a Time

Photography
by Barbara Raué
2015

Series Name:
Cruising Ontario

Book 97: Orillia

Cover photo: Second Empire building - see Page 20

Series Name: Cruising Ontario
Saving Our History One Photo at a Time
in colour photos

Other Books by Barbara Raue

Coins of Gold

Arrows, Indians and Love

The Life and Times of Barbara
Volume 1: Inventions That Have Enhanced My Life
Volume 2: Entertainment That I Have Enjoyed
Volume 3: East Coast Trips
Volume 4: Olympics Have Always Intrigued Me
Volume 5: Wonders of the World
Volume 6: Caribbean Cruises We Have Enjoyed
Volume 7: Animals
Volume 8: Storms and Other Major Disasters in My Lifetime
Volume 9: Wars, Terrorist Attacks and Major Disasters

The Cromwell Family Book

Laura Secord Discovered

Visit Barbara's website to view all of her books
http://barbararaue.ca

Orillia is located in Central Ontario between Lake Couchiching and Lake Simcoe, 135 kilometres (84 miles) north of Toronto. Both lakes are part of the Trent-Severn Waterway. Travel north on Lake Couchiching, then through three locks and the only marine railway in North America leads to Georgian Bay on Lake Huron. Travelling south-east across Lake Simcoe, through many locks (including two of the highest hydraulic lift locks in the world) eventually leads to Lake Ontario. From either of these Great Lakes one can connect to the St. Lawrence and then to the Atlantic Ocean.

The history of what is today the City of Orillia dates back at least several thousand years. Archaeologists have uncovered evidence of fishing by the Huron and Iroquois peoples in the area over 4,000 years ago. The site of an Ojibwa reserve from 1830 to 1838, Orillia subsequently prospered as an agricultural and lumbering community. Early history of the area includes visits from Samuel de Champlain nearly 400 years ago, in the early 17th century. The following century, fur traders and explorers travelled the area extensively.

Due to logging and rail links with Toronto and Georgian Bay, Orillia became a commercial centre and summer resort in the mid-1800s. William Tudhope opened a blacksmith shop in 1864 at Andrew and Colborne Streets. By the end of the century, William's son James headed the Tudhope Carriage Company as part of a conglomerate of businesses. In 1866, Thomas Mulcahy launched his mercantile career in dry goods with the opening of his California Store. Mulcahy and his sons were responsible for the construction of many of Orillia's dwellings and commercial buildings. Andrew Tait was the President of the Huntsville Lumber Company. Tait was a major employer and said to be Orillia's first millionaire. Orillia was founded as a village in 1867 and incorporated as a town in 1875.

Across Lake Couchiching, John Thomson opened his Longford saw milling operation in 1868, using Orillia as a shipping base. By 1900, Orillia was one of the most bustling towns in Ontario. Many of the commercial and residential buildings erected and still standing used red brick trimmed with limestone quarried from Longford.

The town boasted the best Opera House north of Toronto and industrial growth almost unparalleled in the province. With the expansion of the railways, thousands arrived each summer for picnics and holidaying at Couchiching Park.

While there are no records clearly indicating the reason for the name Orillia, the most common explanation holds that the name originates in the Spanish, "orilla," which can mean the shore of either a lake or river. Initial interest in Orillia came from fur traders who used the gathering place at the Narrows to do business with the many tribes that came there each spring and fall. Subsequently, Orillia's economics has ranged from farming (even downtown) to machinery, to automobiles and even one of the first "campers" (a pop-up tent in a car).

In 1912, Orillia was the first municipality in North America to introduce daylight saving time and had the first municipal hydro electric transmission plant in North America. This energy powered an industrial boom with sawmills, iron foundries, and a host of manufacturing companies producing farm implements, carriages, and automobiles and shipping these products across Canada. Orillia also boasted the best Opera House north of Toronto. With the expansion of the railways, thousands arrived each summer for picnics and holidaying at Couchiching Park. In 1912 Orillia printed its own money during the Great Depression as a form of relief.

In Stephen Leacok's 1912 book *Sunshine Sketches of a Little Town*, Orillia was used as the basis for the fictional town known as "Mariposa". The book was based on Leacock's experiences in the town and the city has since the book's release attempted to mimic the fictional location in as many ways as possible. Orillia is known as the "Sunshine City". The Stephen Leacock Museum is a National Historic Site in Orillia.

William E. Bell's 1989 novel *Five Days of the Ghost* was set in Orillia with many readers recognizing popular local spots, including the Guardian Angels Catholic Church, the Samuel de Champlain statue in Couchiching Beach Park and Big Chief Island in the middle of Lake Couchiching. Orillia is also known as the birthplace of Gordon Lightfoot.

During World War II, Orillia produced munitions and aircraft parts at plants that later began manufacturing equipment for the mining and pulp and paper industry.

Orillia was incorporated as a city in 1969. Today, Orillia is as popular a vacation spot as it was a century ago and proudly celebrates its heritage by working hard to preserve historic properties in the downtown. It owns three of the most prominent and attractive 19th-century buildings in the core - the landmark Orillia Opera House, the Sir Sam Steele Memorial Building and Central Public School.

G.W.B. Rope & Twine, one of the foremost North American producers of braided rope from 1973–1985, was also the inventor of the automotive grocery or cargo restraint net. The net was introduced with the launch of the Ford Taurus at Christmas 1985, and shortly thereafter the company was sold and became Polytech Netting Industries, which employed several hundred people until moving to Mexico in 1996-7.

Orillia's "Arts District" is located on Peter Street South, between Mississauga Street East and Colborne Street East and is home to a variety of art galleries, fine dining and shops. At its centre is The Orillia Museum of Art and History (OMAH) playing an instrumental role in municipal cultural events. The museum occupies all four floors of the historic Sir Sam Steele Building, a landmark destination for both residents and visitors. A collection of over 10 000 artefacts of regional historical significance are featured in rotating exhibits.

Many tourists and boaters are attracted to the city each year because of its waterfront Couchiching Beach Park/Centennial Park/Port of Orillia and its position as a gateway to Lake Country, cottage country in Muskoka and Algonquin Provincial Park. The city's waterfront has an extensive lakeshore boardwalk, two beaches, several playgrounds, an outdoor theatre, a touring ferry, and a children's train.

The main administration offices for the City of Orillia are located at 50 Andrew Street South, Suite 300. The administration offices are in the Tudhope building which has a long history of industrial operations dating back to the beginning of the 20th century, when it housed the carriage and automobile manufacturing operations of the Tudhope Motor Company. In July of 1997, the City of Orillia established its municipal offices in the western half of the refurbished downtown factory. In 2001, this part of the building was designated under the Ontario Heritage Act as a property of cultural heritage value.

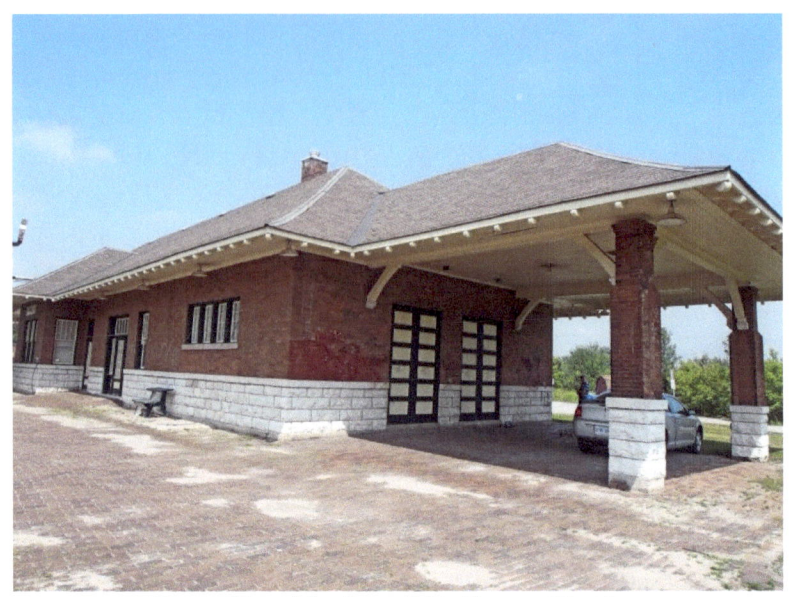

Canadian National Railway Station

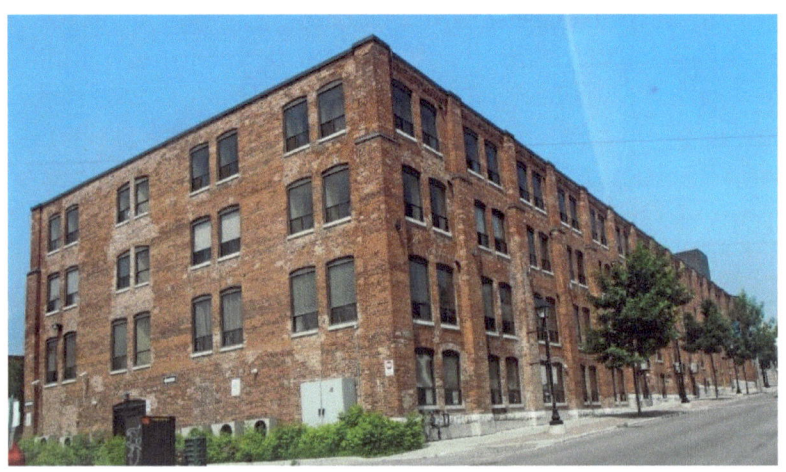

Factory building – red brick

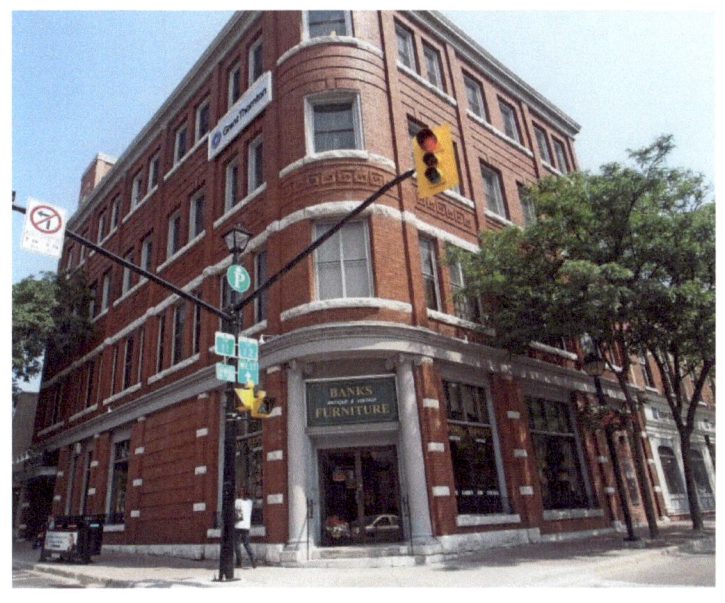

Corner of West Street North and Mississauga Street West

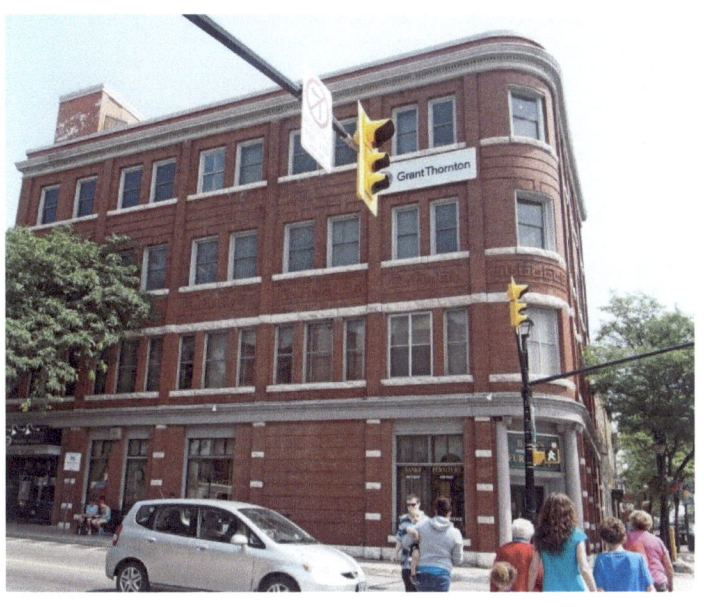

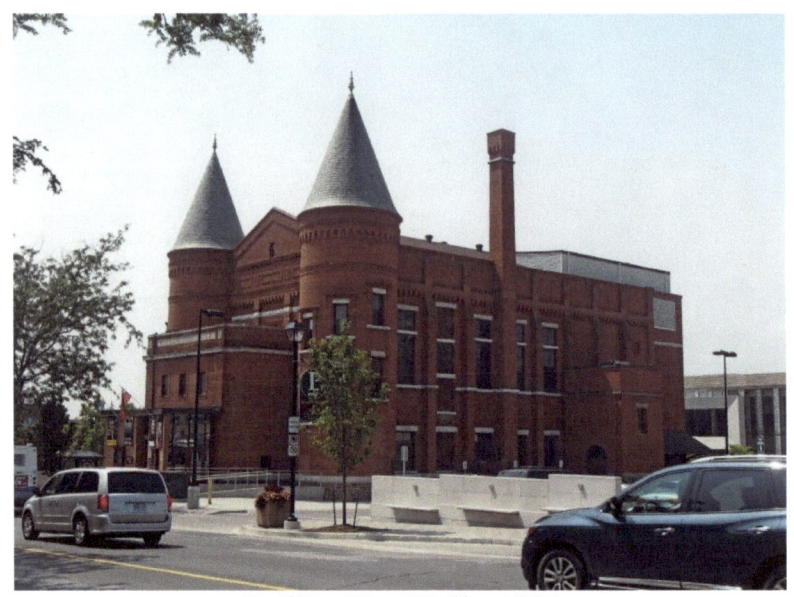
Orillia City Hall - 1894

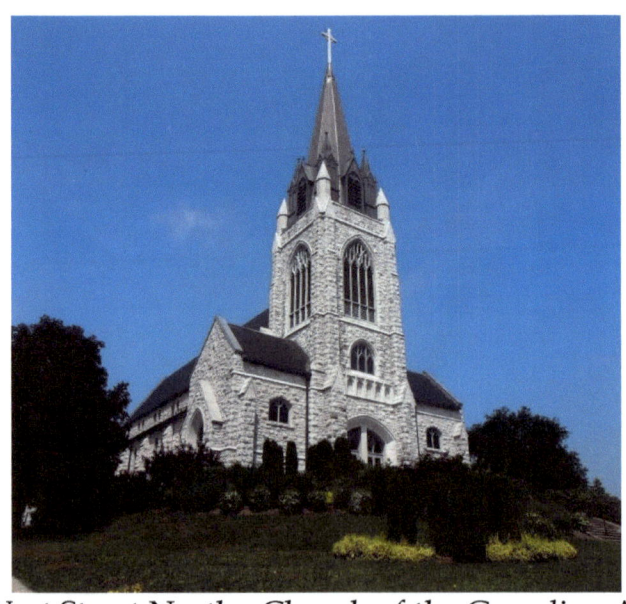
115 West Street North - Church of the Guardian Angels

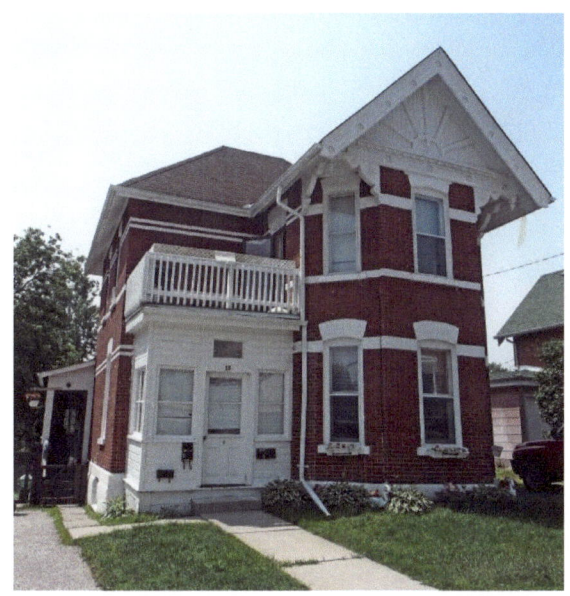

#19 - Gothic Revival – verge board trim on gable, fretwork

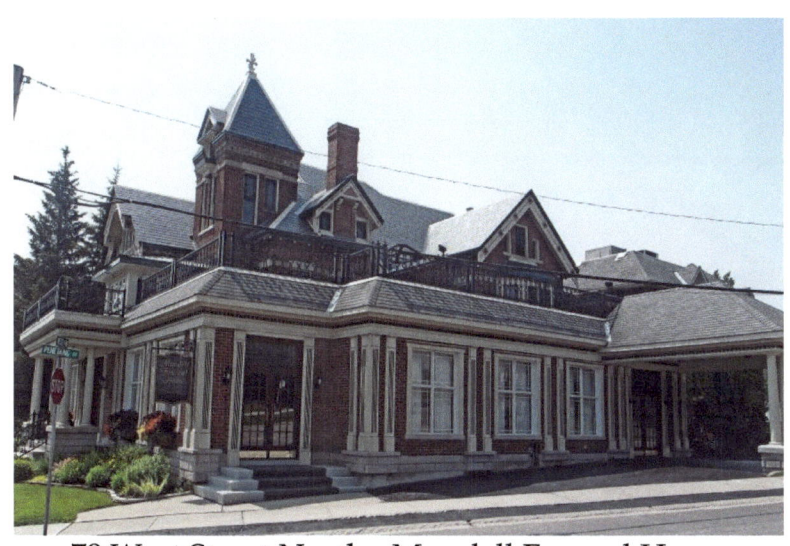

79 West Street North - Mundell Funeral Home
Queen Anne style, second floor balcony

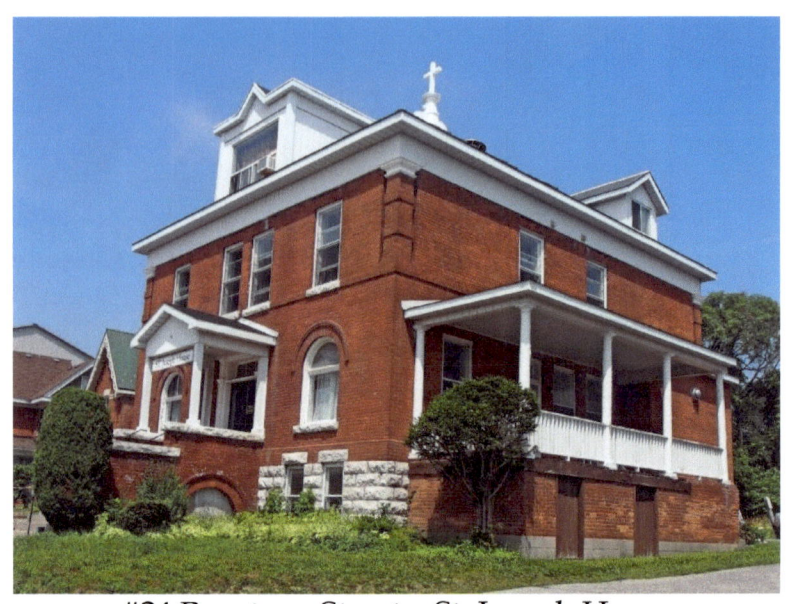

#24 Penetang Street – St. Joseph House
Catholic Family Services of Simcoe County

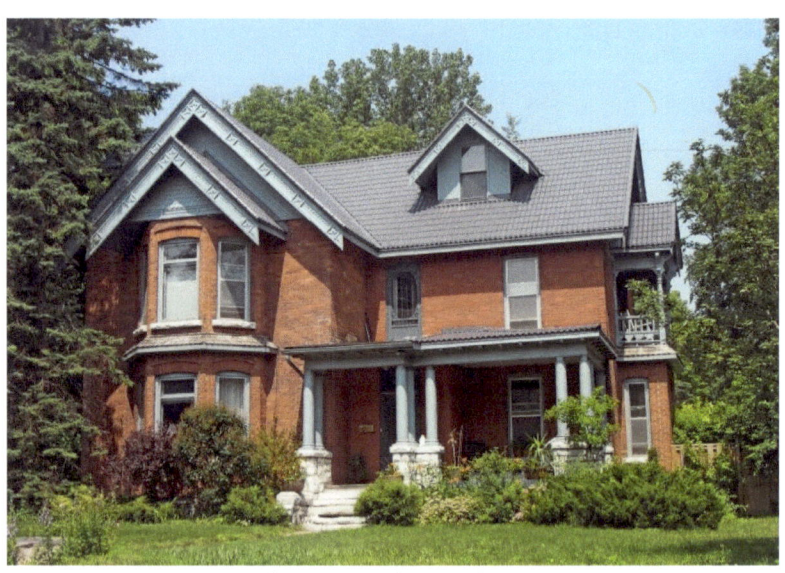

Two-storey bay window, dormer in attic,
balcony on end on second floor

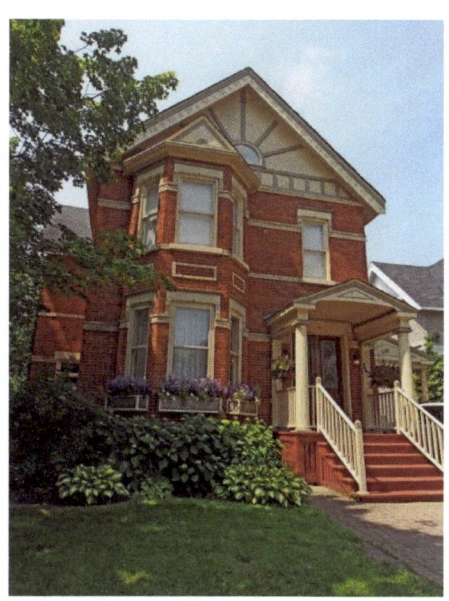

#143 – Gothic Revival, two-storey bay window, pediment above porch, Tudor accents on gable

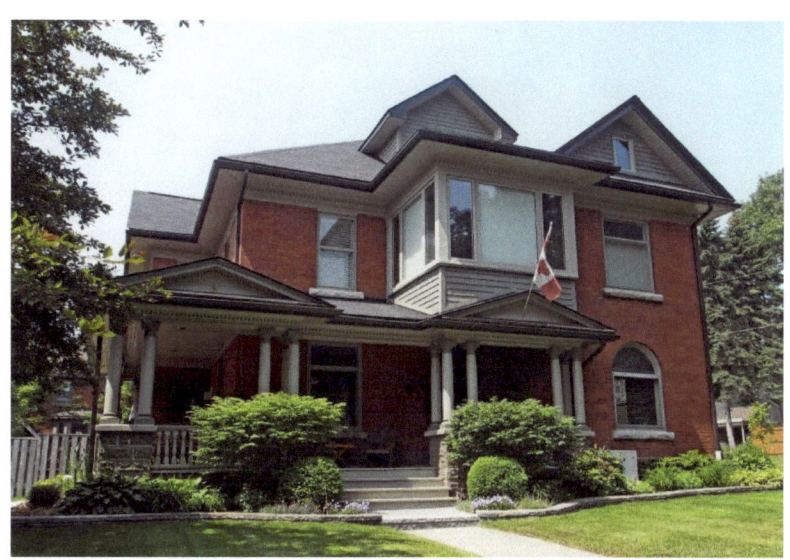

#159 – Edwardian style, dormer in attic above added room above verandah, pediments, wraparound verandah

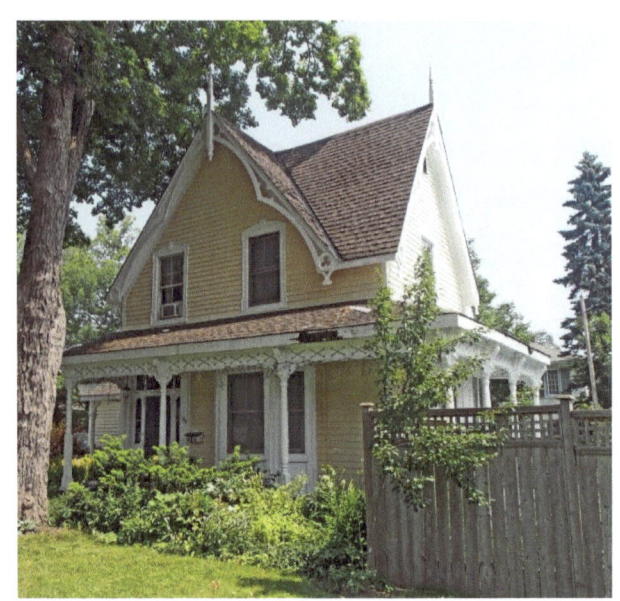

#160 – Gothic Revival, finials and verge board trim on gables

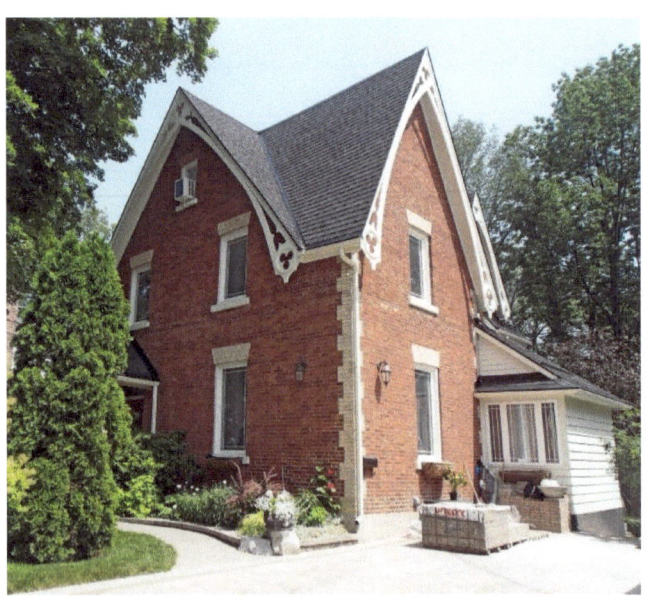

Gothic Revival, verge board trim, corner quoins

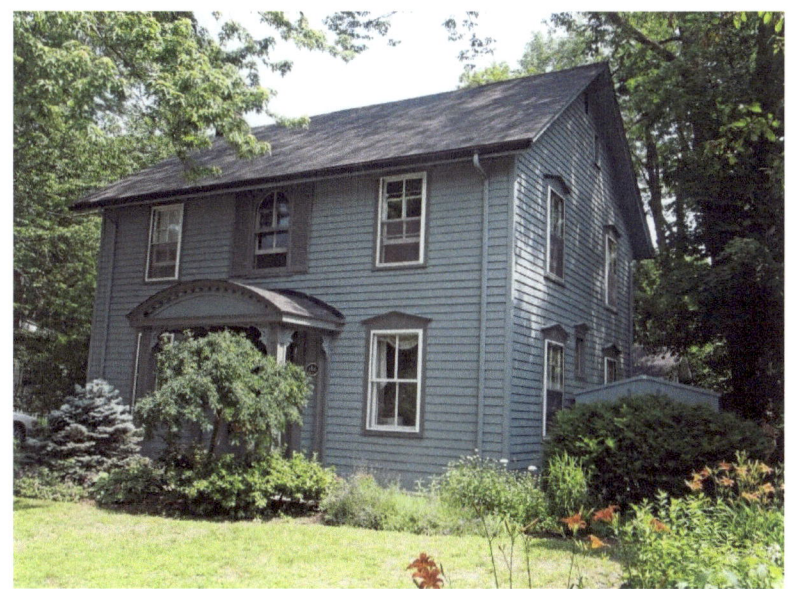

#186

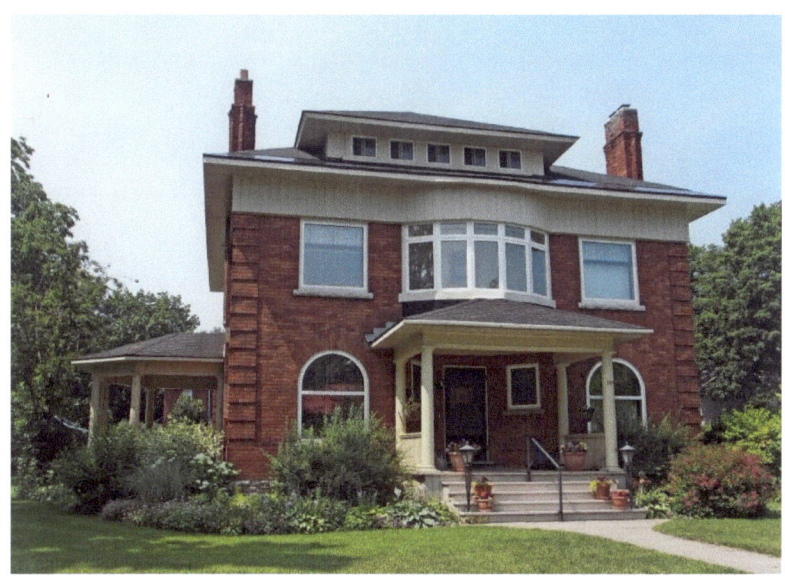

#199 – Italianate - dormer in attic, second floor bay window

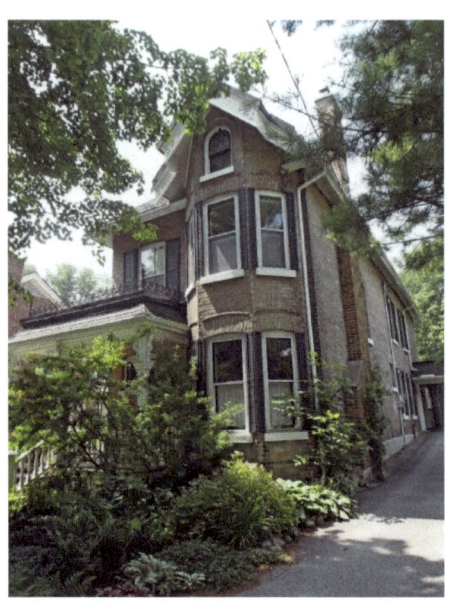

Gothic Revival, yellow brick, iron cresting above porch, two-and-a-half storey bay window

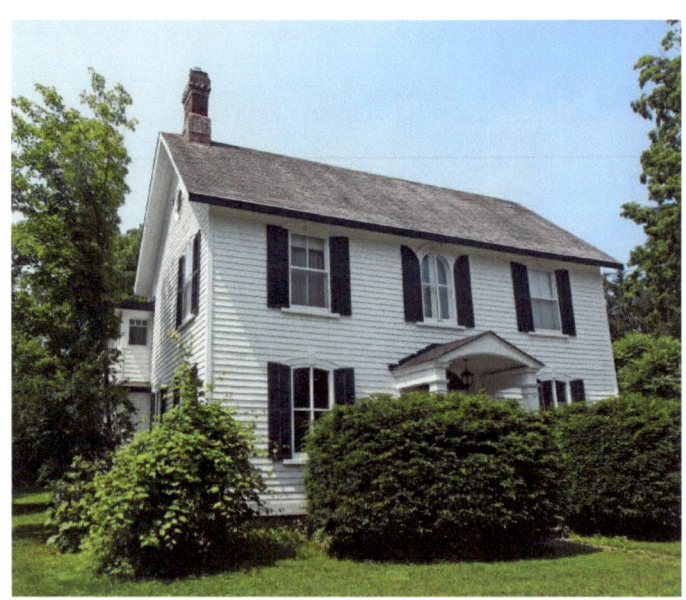

Georgian style

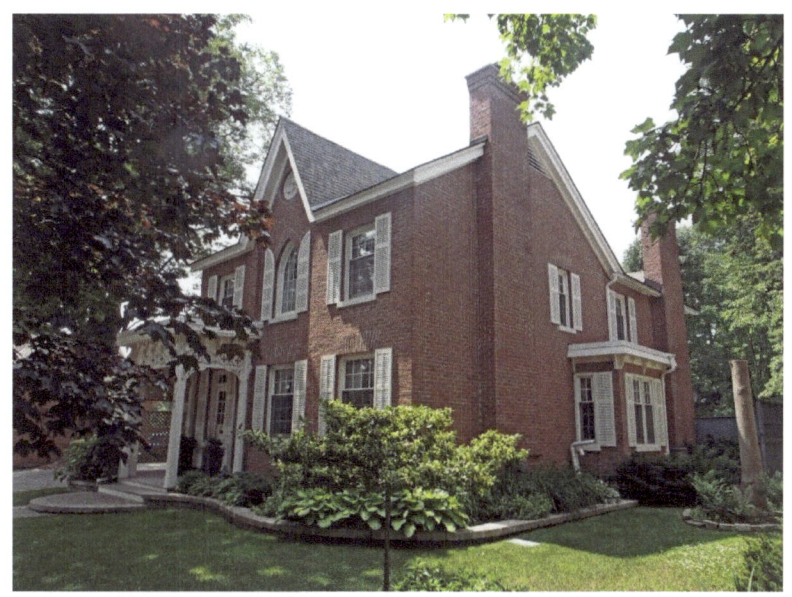

Gothic Revival – red brick

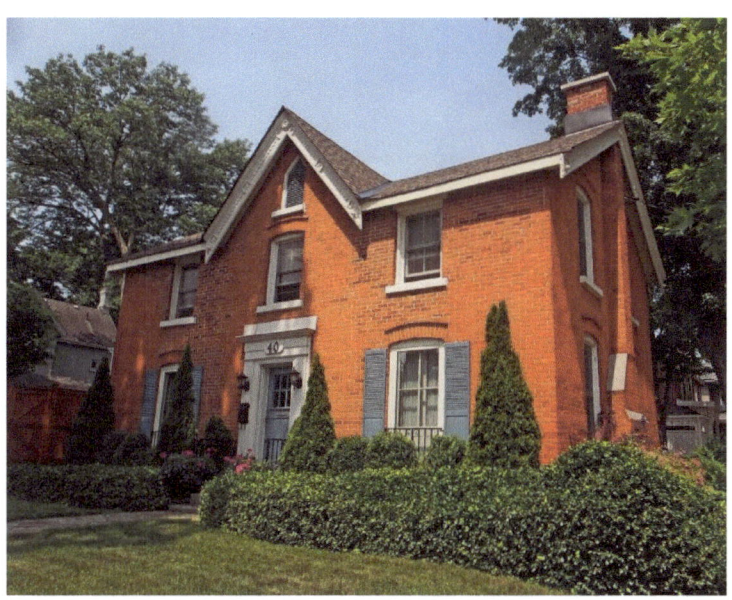

#40 – Gothic revival, verge board trim

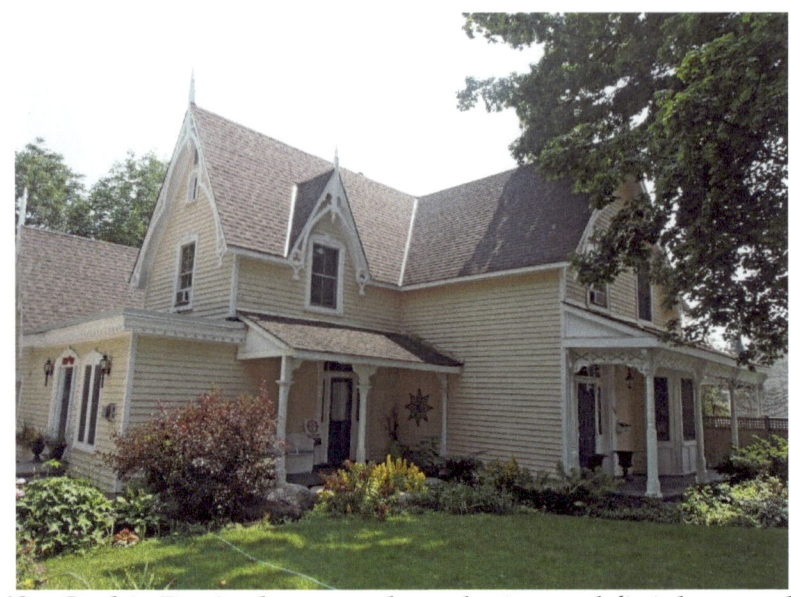

#160 - Gothic Revival – verge board trim and finials on gables

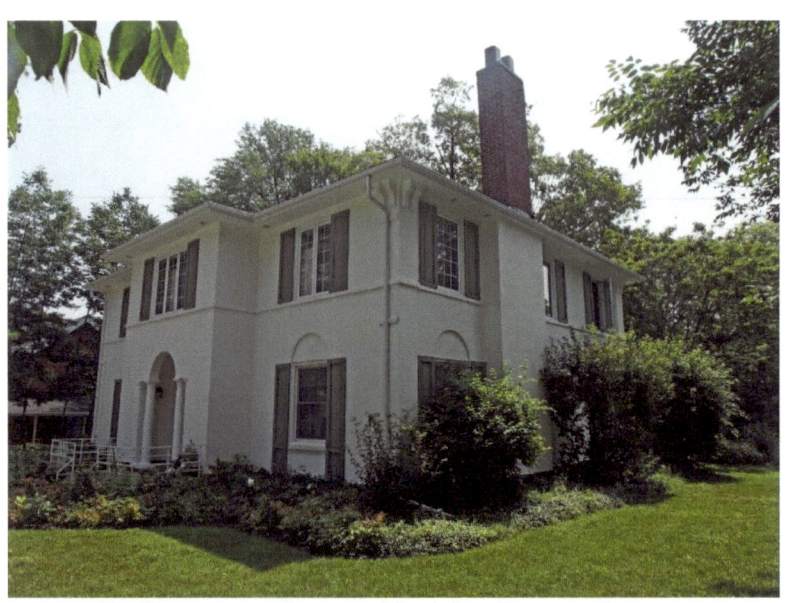

Italianate style – red brick plastered over

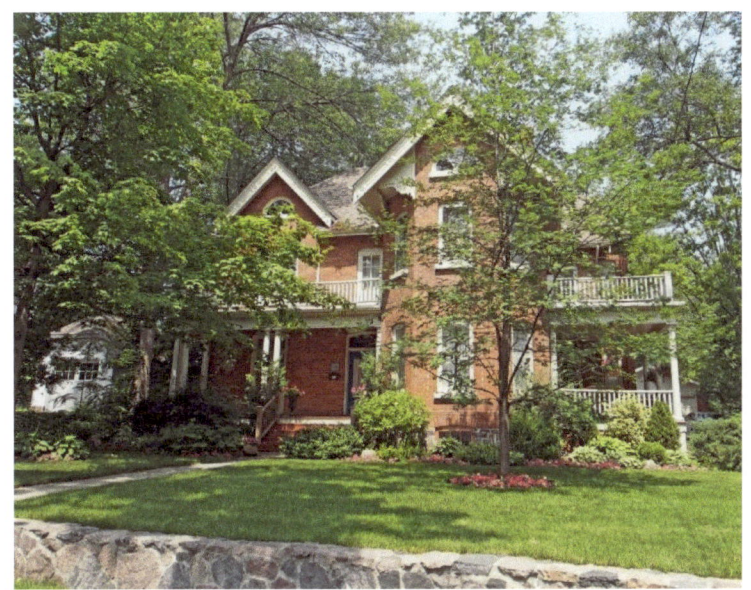

Gothic Revival

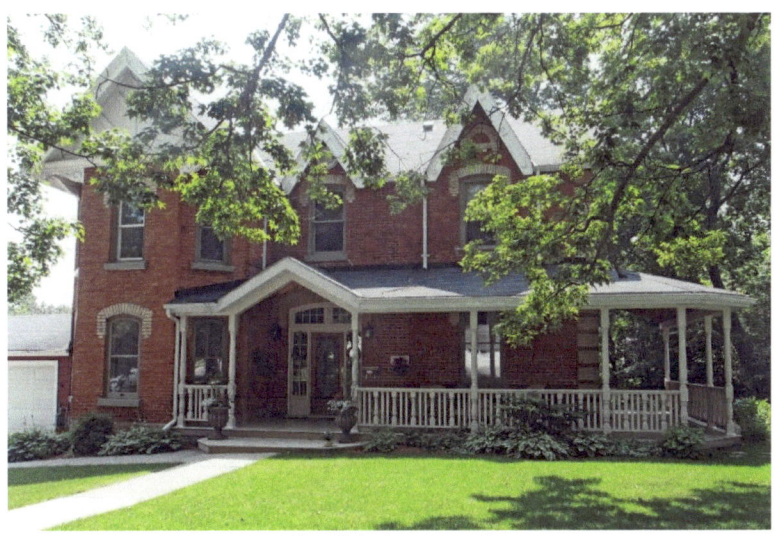

Gothic Revival

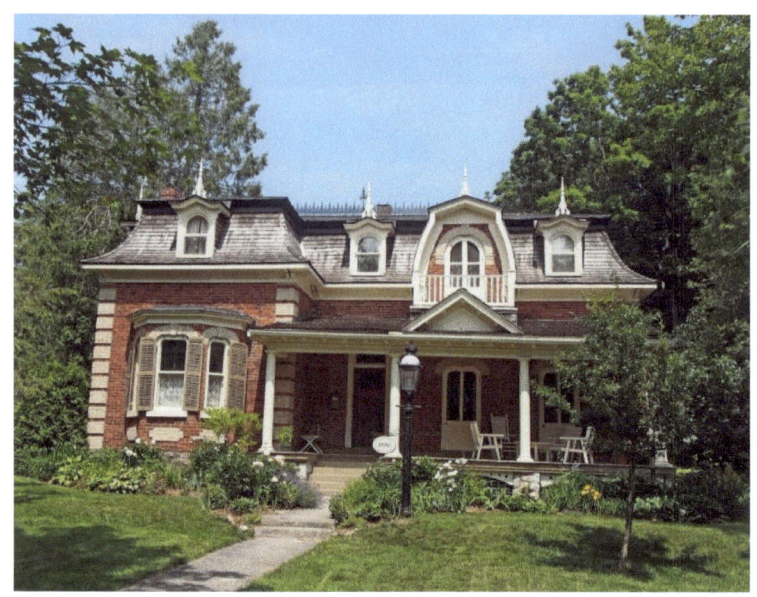

#84 – E.J. McCrohan, Harness Maker c. 1880
Second Empire style, mansard roof, iron cresting around roof,
finials on dormers, second floor balcony, corner quoins

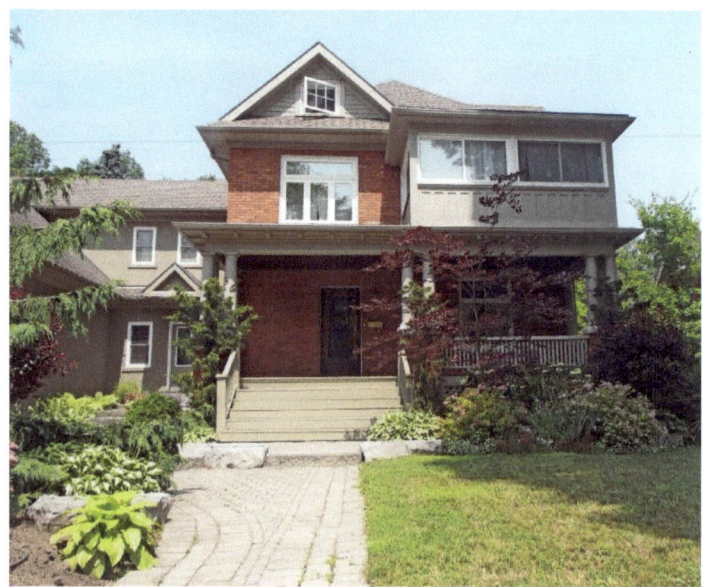

#99 - Edwardian

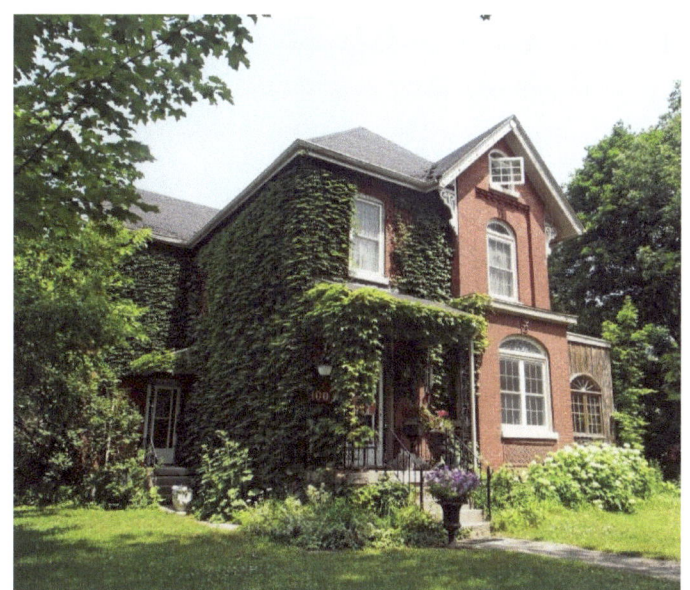

#100 – Gothic Revival, fretwork under eaves
Dentil moulding, keystones

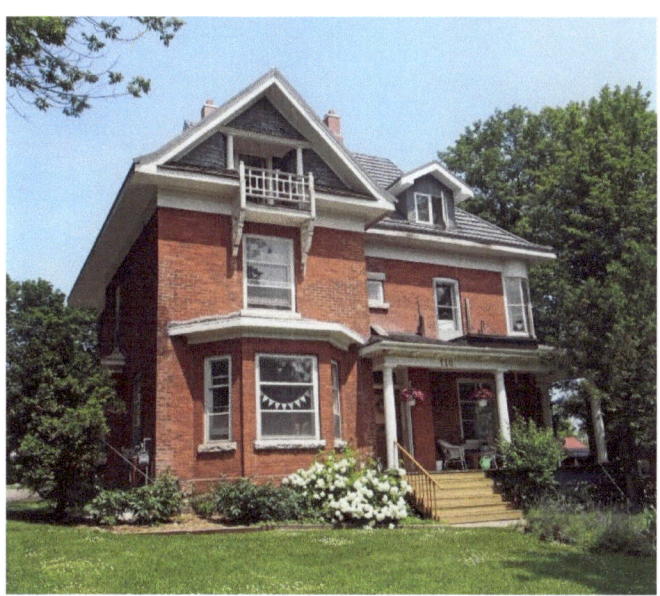

#110 - Edwardian, bay window, dormer in attic

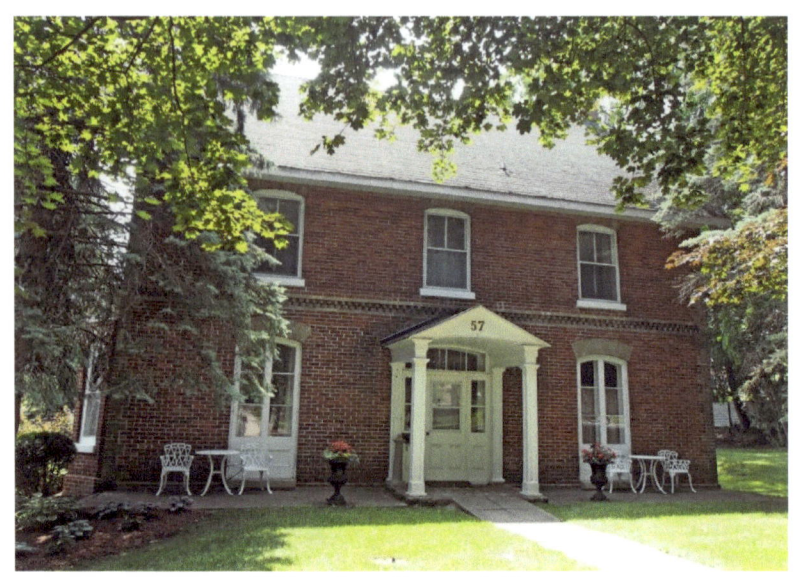

#57 – dentil moulding

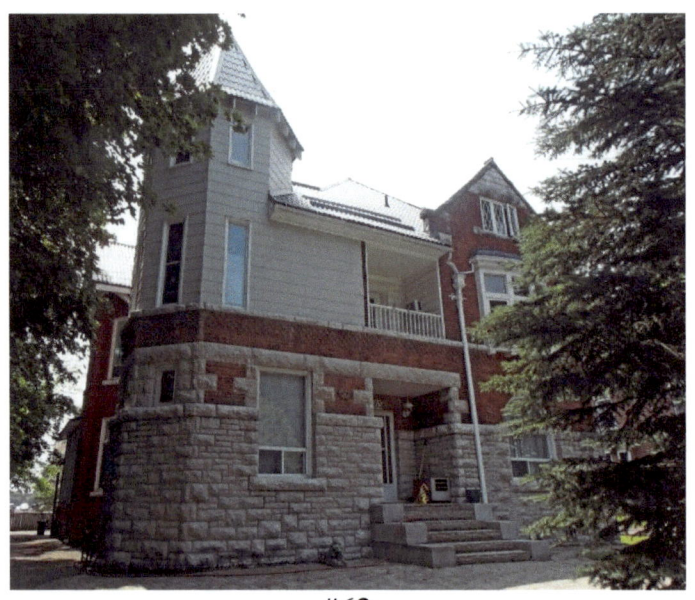

#63

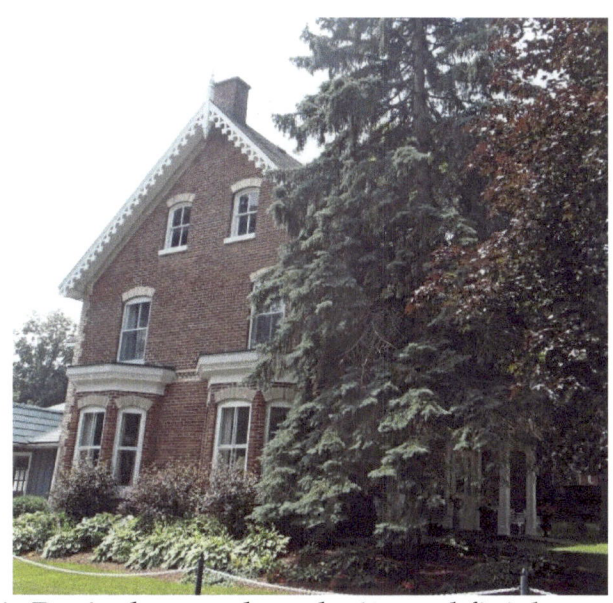

Gothic Revival, verge board trim and finials on gable,
bay windows

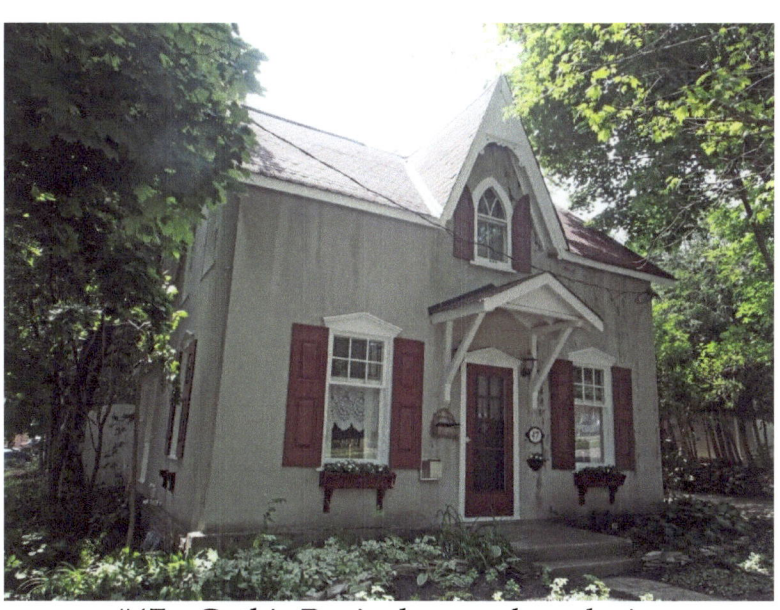

#47 – Gothic Revival, verge board trim

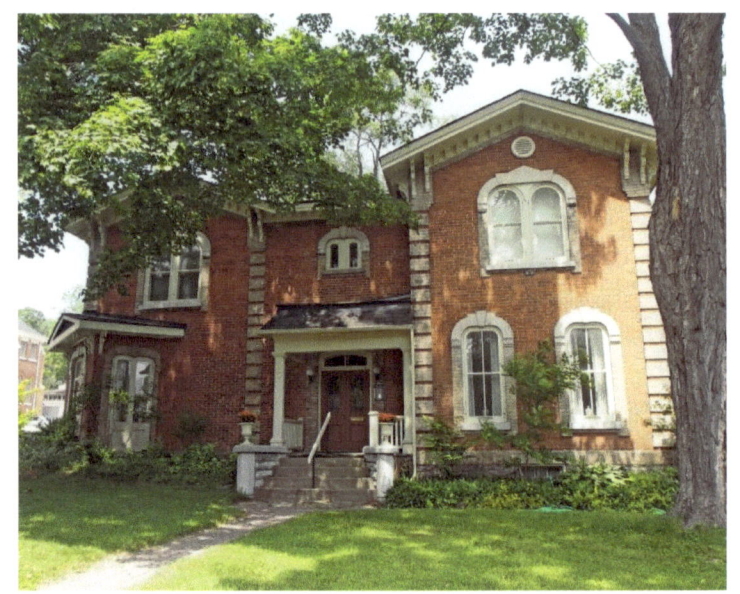

#42 – Gothic Revival, corner quoining, cornice brackets

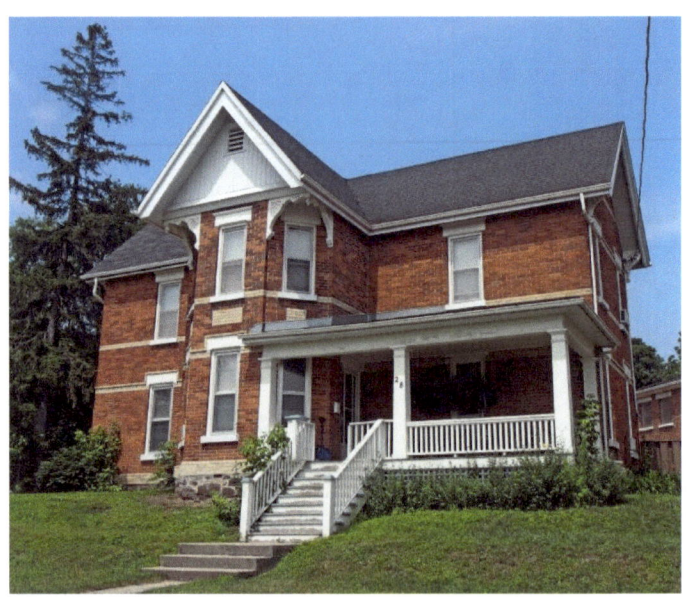

Two-storey tower-like bay, fretwork

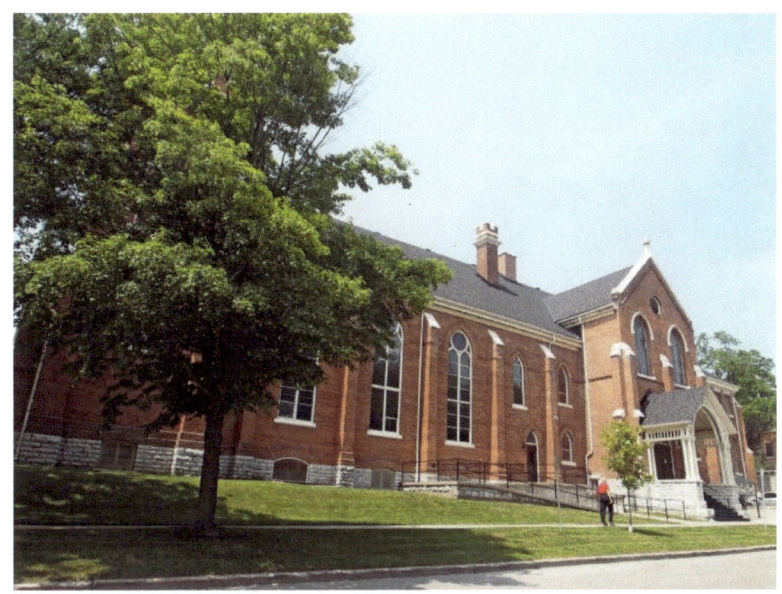

99 Peter Street North - St. Andrew's Presbyterian Church –
erected 1888 - Lancet windows, buttresses

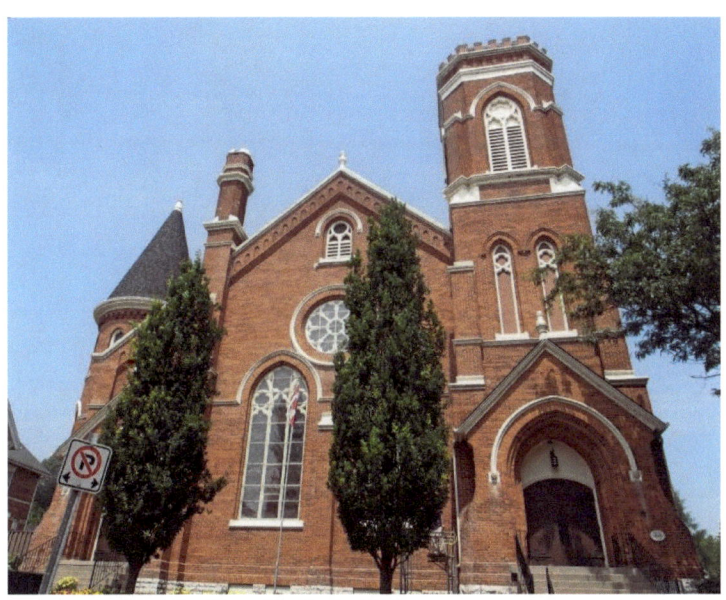

Gothic Revival, bell tower and turret

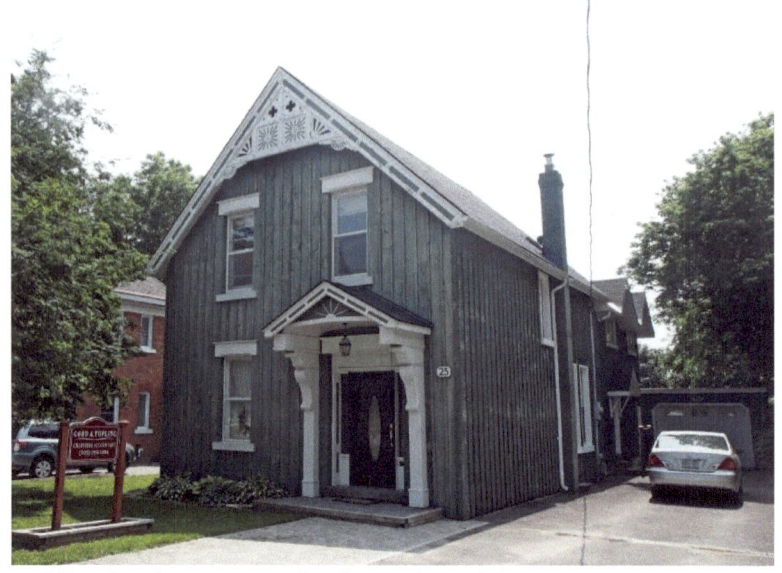

#25 - Gothic Revival – board and batten construction

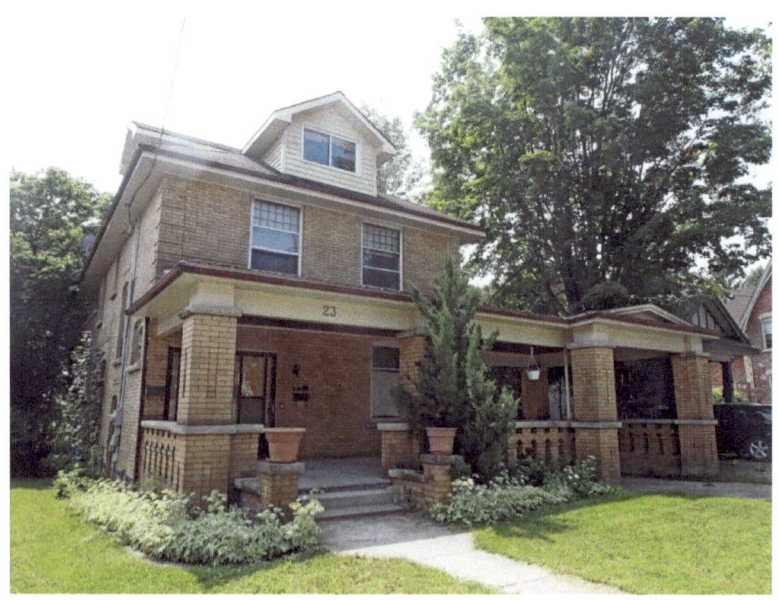

#23 - Italianate, dormer in attic, corner quoins

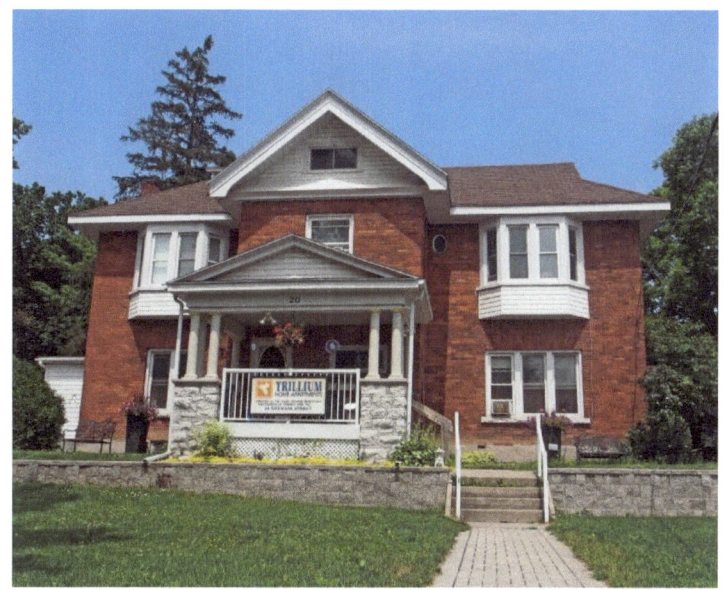

#20 - Edwardian, pediment, second floor bay windows

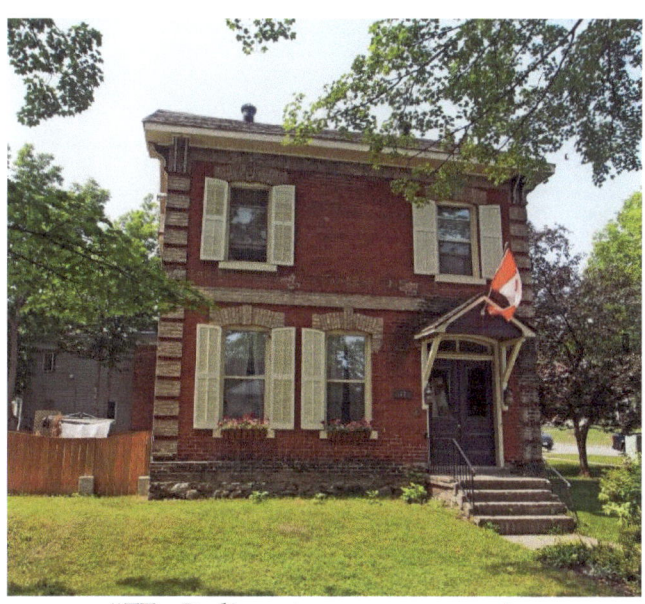

#77 - Italianate – corner quoins

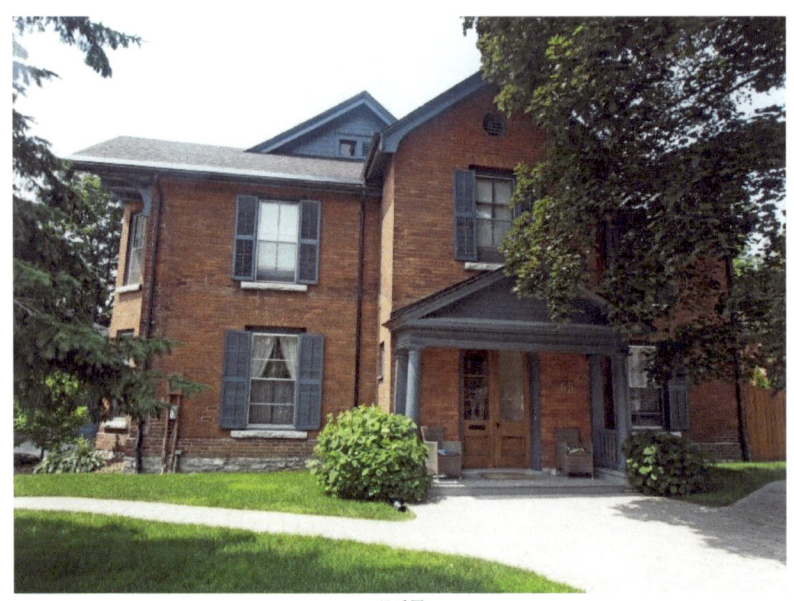

#65

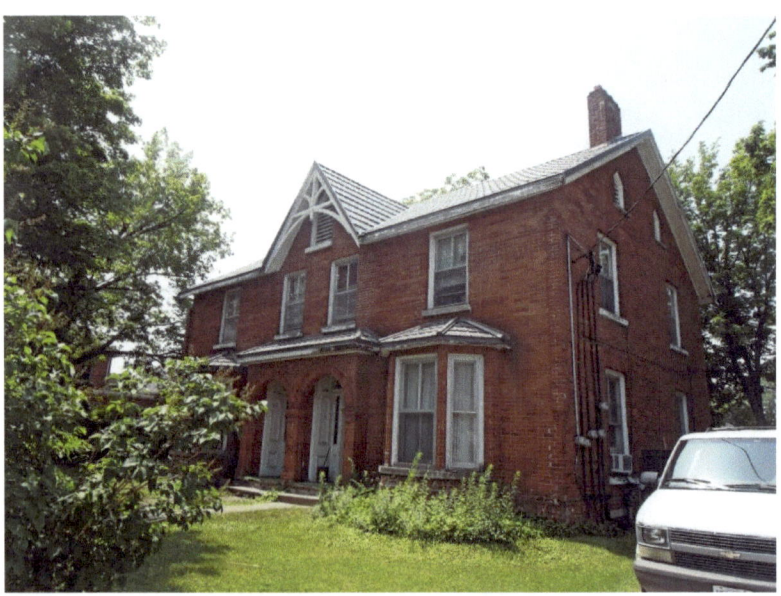

Gothic Revival, verge board trim on gable, rectangular bay windows on first floor

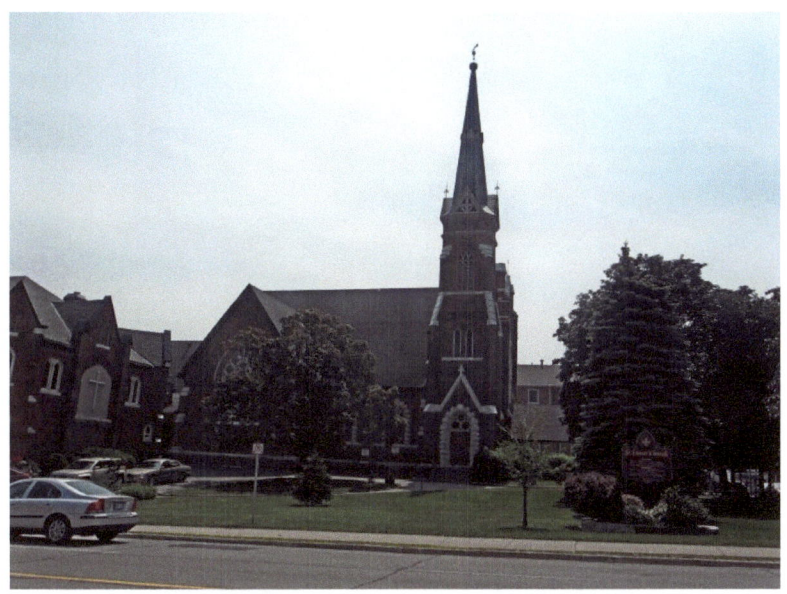

58 Peter Street North - St. James' Anglican Church,
buttresses, rose window, lancet windows

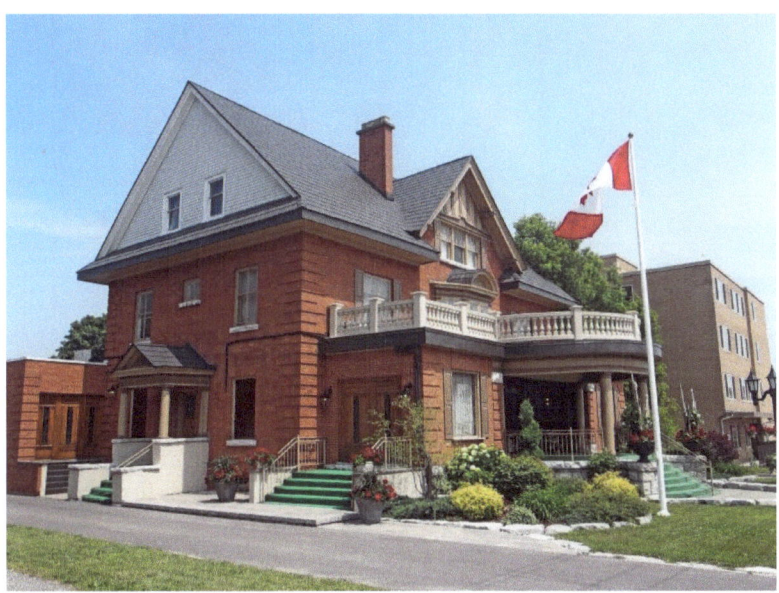

54 Coldwater Street East - Carson Funeral Homes, L. Doolittle
Chapel - Gothic Revival, pediment above side entrance,
balcony on second floor, Tudor accents on front gable

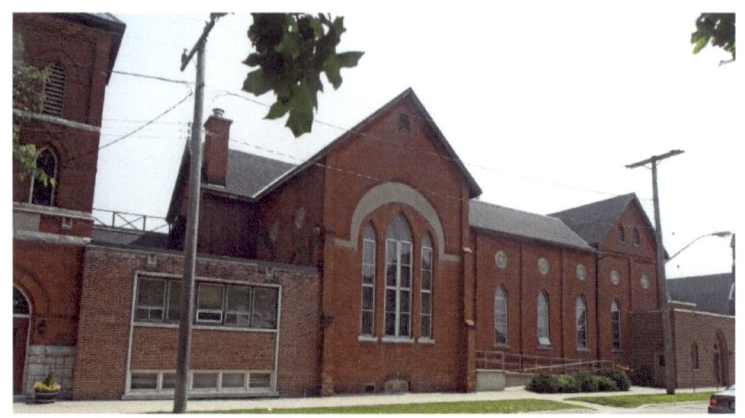

St. Paul's United Church – buttresses, lancet windows

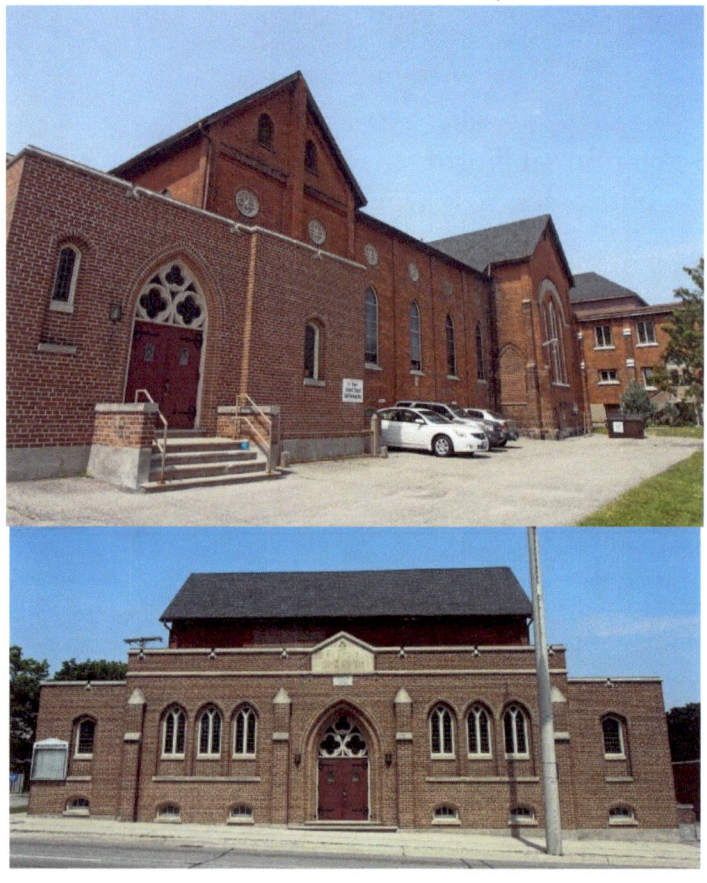

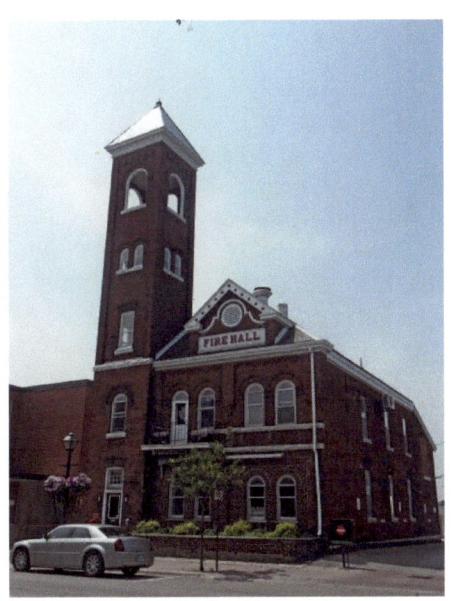

27 Peter Street North – old Fire Hall

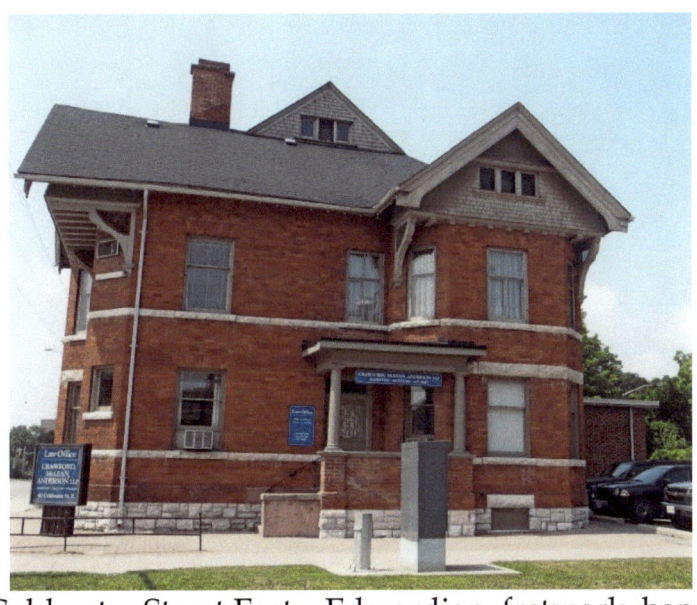

40 Coldwater Street East – Edwardian, fretwork, banding

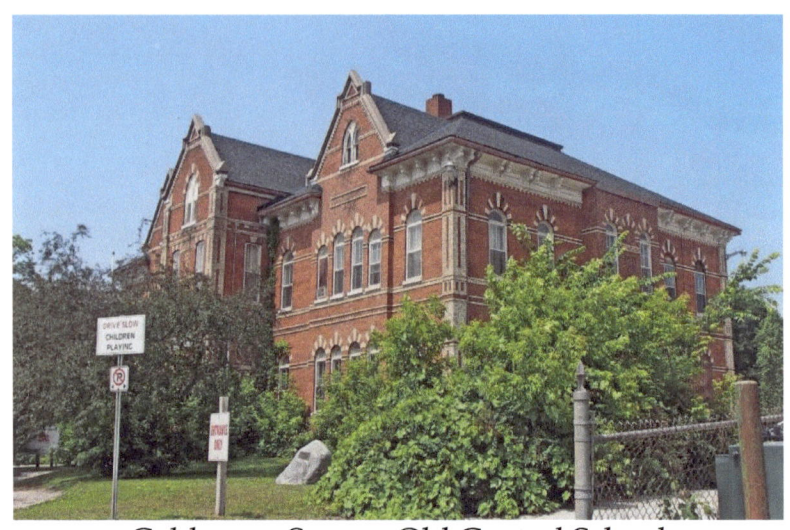

Coldwater Street - Old Central School
cornice brackets, dichromatic brickwork

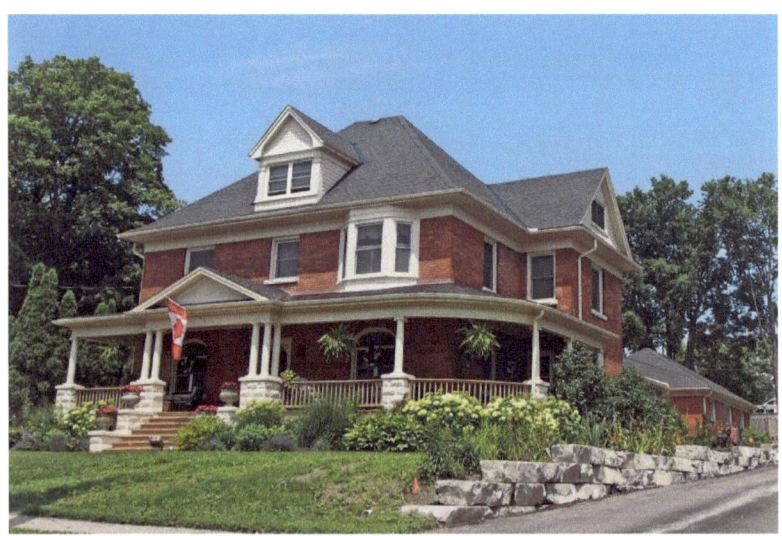

Edwardian, dormer in attic, pediment above wraparound
verandah, second floor bay window

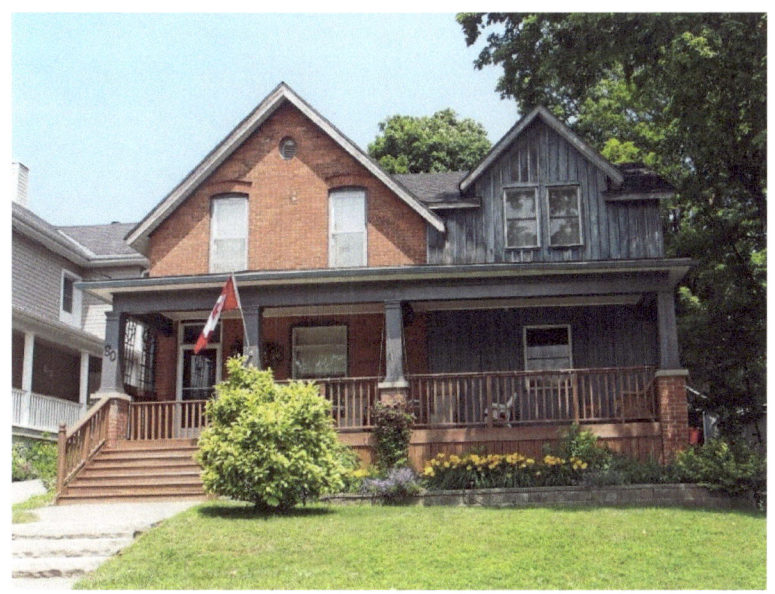

#80 - Gothic Revival

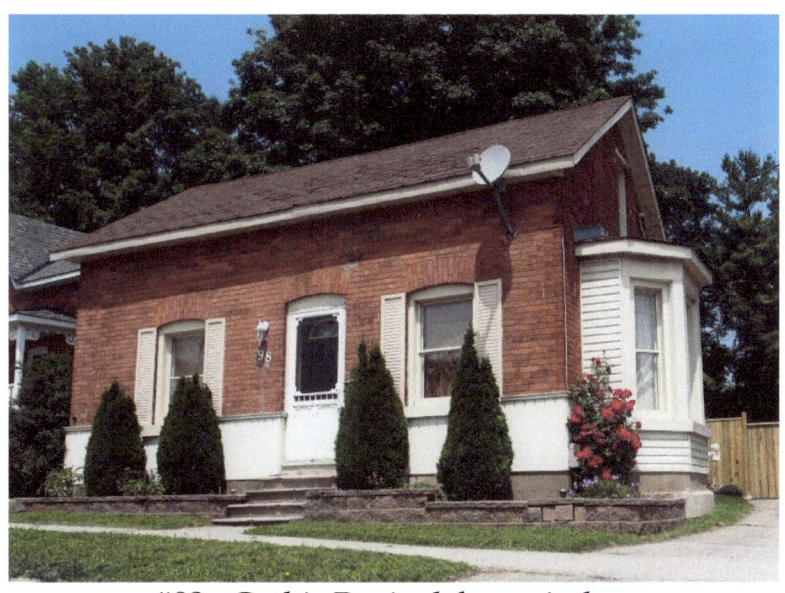

#98 - Gothic Revival, bay window

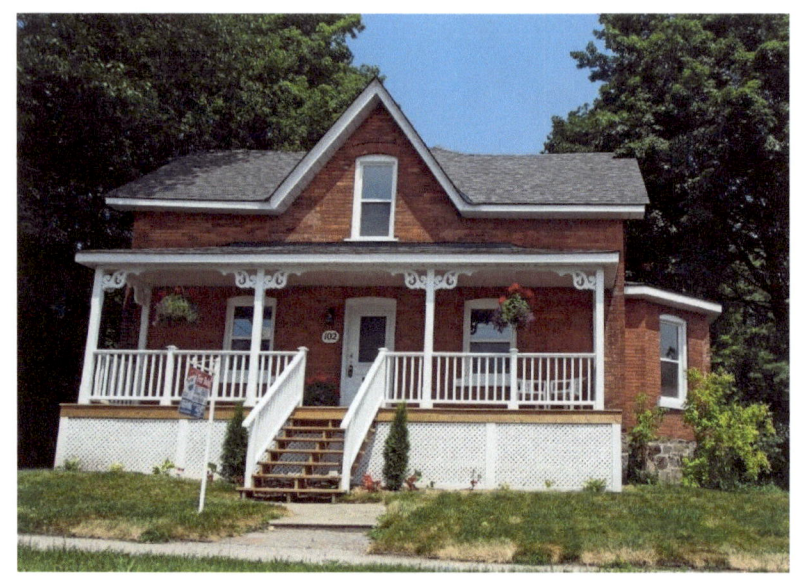

#102 - Gothic Revival

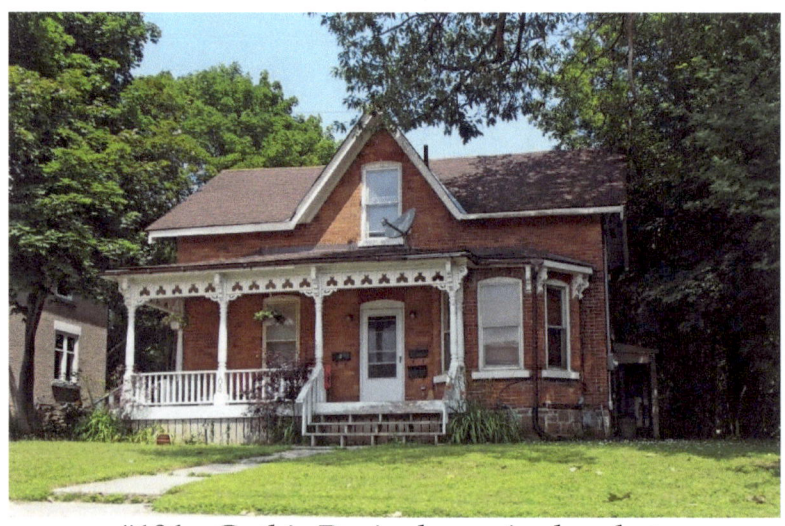

#106 – Gothic Revival, cornice brackets

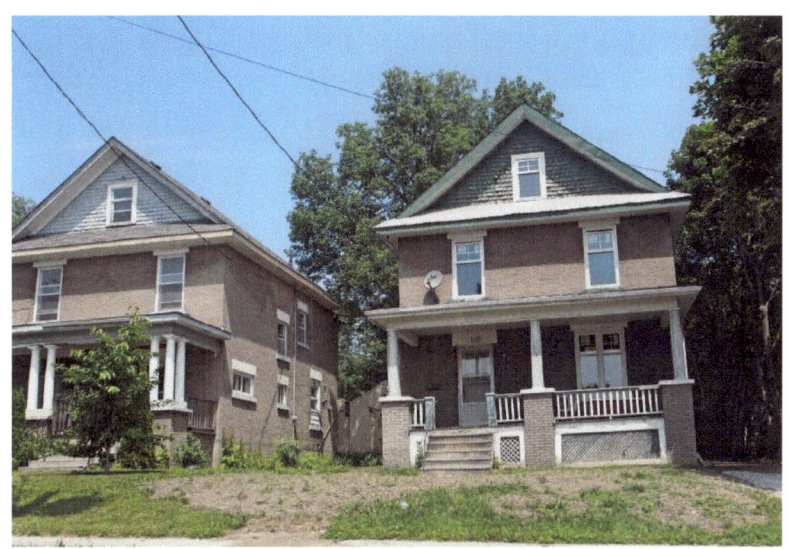

#110 – Edwardian

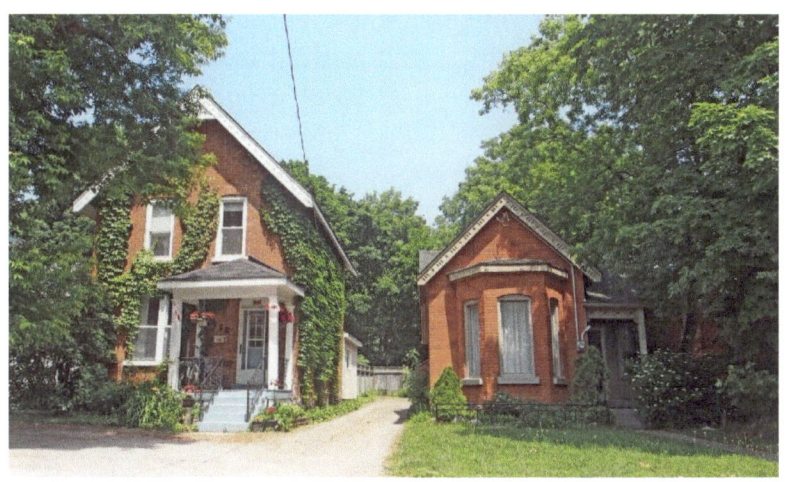

#148 and #146 – Gothic Revival – bay window

Banding: Different materials, colours or textures used in horizontal bands along a wall. Example: old Central School – see Page 32	
Brackets: a decorative or weight-bearing structural element which forms a right angle with one side against a wall and the other under a projecting surface such as an eave or roof. Example: see Page 34	
Buttress: a masonry structure built against or projecting from a wall which serves to support or reinforce the wall. In Canadian architecture, they are sometimes used for decoration. Example: St. Andrew's Presbyterian Church, see Page 25	
Cornice: originally the wooden overhang of the roof. With the use of stone, brick, iron and steel, the cornice is any projecting shelf at the top of a ceiling or roof. They can be very decorative. Example: see Page 25	
Dentil Moulding: an even series of rectangles used as ornamental decoration in cornices. Example: see Page 21	
Dichromatic brickwork: the use of two colours of brick, tile or slate to decorate a façade. Example: Old Central School, see Page 32	

Dormer: (French for "sleep") a gable end window that pierces through the plane of a sloping roof surface to create usable space in the top floor or attic of a building by adding headroom. Example: see Page 12	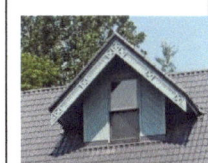
Fretwork: interlaced decorative design resembling a bracket Example: see Page 24	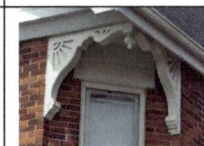
Gable: the triangular portion of a wall between the edges of a sloping roof. Example: see Page 17	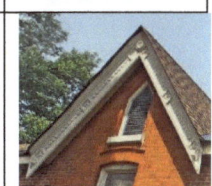
Iron Cresting: A decorative ornament along the top of a roof. Iron cresting was popular in the Baroque era and also in Italianate, Victorian, Second Empire and Queen Anne styles of architecture. Example: see Page 20	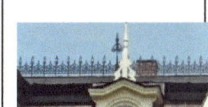
Keystones and Voussoirs: a voussoir is a wedge-shaped element used in building an arch. A keystone is the central stone that locks all the stones into position, allowing the arch to bear weight. A keystone is often enlarged and embellished. Example: see Page 21	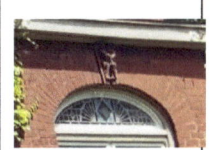
Lancet Window: a tall, narrow window with a pointed arch at its top. Example: see Page 29	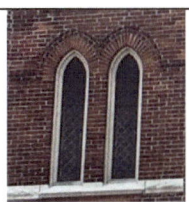

Mansard Roof: This style was popularized by Francois Mansart (1598-1666), an accomplished architect of the French Baroque period and especially fashionable during the Second French Empire (1852-1870). This roof is almost flat on the top section, with two slopes on each of its sides with the lower slope at a steeper angle than the upper and having dormer windows. Example: see Page 20	
Pediment: a triangular section above the horizontal structure (entablature), typically supported by columns. The inside of the triangle is called the tympanum. Example: see Page 27	
Quoin: masonry blocks at the corner of a wall, often a decorative feature, usually larger or of a different colour than the rest of the wall.

Example: see Page 14 | |

Rose Window: a circular window with ornamental tracery radiating from the centre. Example: see Page 29	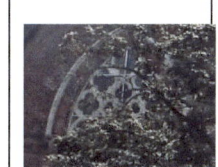
Turret: a small tower that projects from the wall of a building. Example: old City Hall	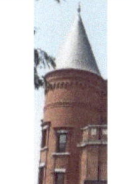
Verge board and Finial: also called bargeboards – hang from the projecting end of a roof and are often elaborately carved and ornamented. **Finial:** ornament added to the top of a gable, pinnacle, canopy or spire – a Gothic element. Example: see Page 18	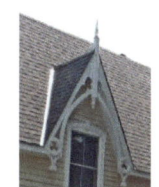

Edwardian, 1900-1930 – This style bridges the ornate and elaborate styles of the Victorian era and the simplified styles of the 20th century. Balanced facades, simple roof lines, dormer windows, large front porches, and smooth brick surfaces are its characteristics. Example: see Page 21	
Georgian, before 1860 – This style began with the British King Georges in the 18th century. These buildings have balanced facades around a central door, medium-pitched gable roofs, and small paned windows. Example: see Page 16	
Gothic Revival, 1830-1890 – These decorative buildings have sharply-pitched gables with highly detailed verge boards, pointed-arch window openings, and dichromatic brickwork. It is a common style in Ontario. Example: see Page 34	
Italianate, 1850-1900 – It has wide-bracketed eaves, belvederes, wrap-around verandahs. Example: see Page 15	

Queen Anne, 1885-1900 – This style is distinguished by an irregular outline featuring a combination of an offset tower, broad gables, projecting two-storey bays, verandahs, multi-sloped roofs, and tall, decorative chimneys. A mixture of brick and wood is common. Windows often have one large single-paned bottom sash and small panes in the upper sash. Example: 79 West Street North, Page 11	
Second Empire, 1860-1880 – The mansard roof is the most noteworthy feature of this style and is evidence of the French origins. Projecting central towers and one or two-storey bays can also be present. Example: see Page 20	
Tudor Revival – exposed timbers with stucco infill, multi-paned windows. Example: see Page 13	

www.ingramcontent.com/pod-product-compliance
Lightning Source LLC
Chambersburg PA
CBHW041142180526
45159CB00002BB/701